Metro Litho
Oak Forest, IL 60452

DATE DUE		

#393

582.16   Jennings, Terry J
JEN   Trees

90031

The Young Scientist Investigates

Trees

by
Terry Jennings

 CHILDRENS PRESS®
CHICAGO

Illustrated by
Norma Burgin
Karen Daws
David More

Library of Congress Cataloging-in-Publication Data

Jennings, Terry J.
    Trees / by Terry Jennings.
        p.   cm. — (The Young scientist investigates)
    Includes index.
    Summary: Discusses the life cycle and individual parts of
trees. Includes study questions, activities, and experiments.
    ISBN 0-516-08444-5
    1. Trees—Juvenile literature. 2. Trees—Experiments—Juvenile
literature. [1. Trees.] I. Title. II. Series: Jennings, Terry J. Young
scientist investigates.
    QK475.8.J46   1989
    582.16—dc 19   88-37552
                                                         CIP
                                                         AC

North American edition published in 1989 by
Childrens Press®, Inc.

© Terry Jennings 1982
First published 1982 by Oxford University Press

Printed in the United States of America
1 2 3 4 5 6 7 8 9 10 R 98 97 96 95 94 93 92 91 90 89

Contents

Trees

Trees are found everywhere. They grow in the country in woods, in fields, and along roads. We can find trees in town parks and yards. Trees also grow in town squares and along the sides of streets. Many schools have trees planted on their grounds.

California Redwood

Trees are large, woody plants. They are the world's biggest plants. The tallest tree still standing is a California redwood tree in California that is 367 feet high. But the record breaker is a fallen eucalyptus tree in Australia that was found to be 525 feet long.

Parts of a tree

On this page there are some common trees. Each kind of tree has a shape of its own. You can often recognize trees by their shapes. It is not always easy to recognize them by their shapes, though, when they grow close together. Many town trees have been trimmed. This also changes their shape so that it is hard to recognize them.

Oak

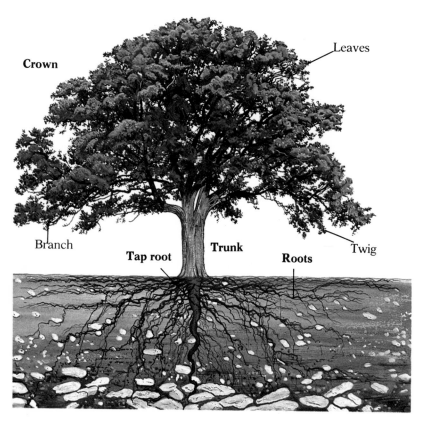

Crown

Leaves

Branch

Tap root

Trunk

Roots

Twig

Ash

All trees have three main parts. There is a thick woody stem called a trunk. The crown of the tree is made up of leaves and branches. The very thin branches are called twigs. At certain times of the year there may be buds, flowers or fruit on the twigs. At the base of the tree there are a large number of spreading roots.

Elm

Roots

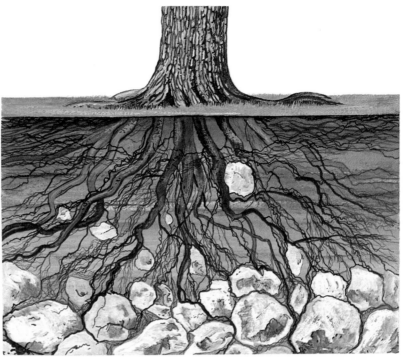

Horse chestnut

Beech

Pine

The roots of a tree are large and branched. Some trees have one big root called a tap root. The tap root grows deep into the soil and has smaller roots growing from it.

Other trees have many large and small roots, like the one in the picture above. Sometimes some of the roots stick out of the ground. The roots almost always spread as far underground as the twigs spread in the crown of the tree. The roots anchor the tree. They stop strong winds from blowing the tree over.

Roots also take up water and mineral salts from the soil. Tree roots take up huge quantities of water. In one day, the roots of a large oak tree may take up well over 53 gallons of water from the soil.

Trunks

The trunk of a tree is made of wood. The trunk has to be strong to support the crown of the tree. The trunk is surrounded by bark that protects the tender growing part of the tree. It is often possible to recognize a tree by its bark.

The trunk carries water and mineral salts from the roots up to the leaves. Food made by the leaves passes down the trunk to the roots. The water, mineral salts and food travel in tiny tubes that make up the wood of the trunk.

If the trunk of a tree is cut right across, we can see rings in the wood. These are called annual rings. A tree grows one ring every year. So by counting the rings we can tell the age of a tree. If the weather is bad one year, the trunk will not grow so much and the ring produced that year will be narrow. If the weather is good, the trunk will grow a lot, and that year's ring will be wider.

Oak bark

Ash bark

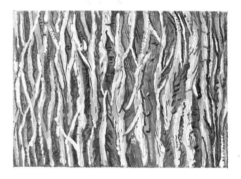

Beech bark

Chestnut bark

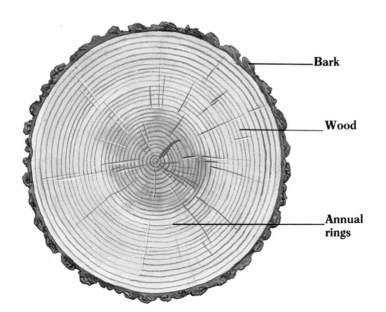

Bark

Wood

Annual rings

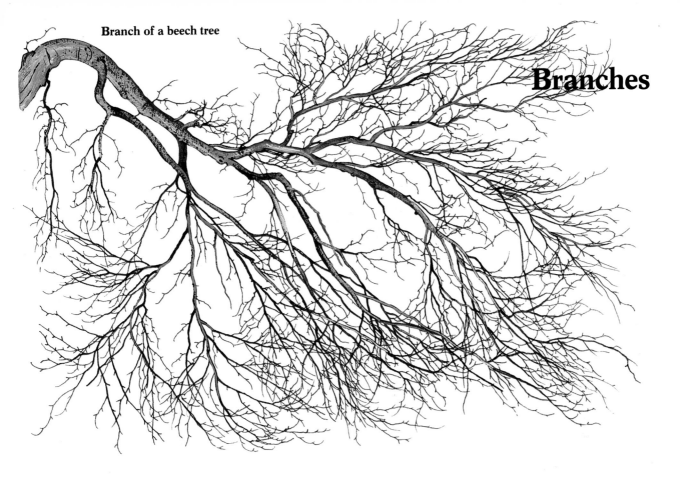

Branch of a beech tree

Branches

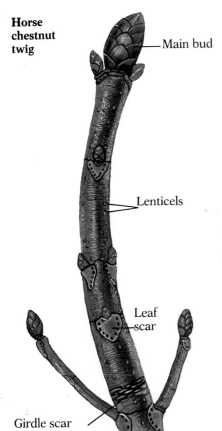

Horse chestnut twig

Main bud

Lenticels

Leaf scar

Girdle scar

Branches grow from the trunk of the tree. These branches make up the crown. The branches are arranged so that as many leaves as possible can receive sunlight. Like the trunk, the branches of a tree are also made of wood.

From the branches grow twigs. Leaves and flowers grow from buds on the twigs. If you look at a twig carefully, you can often see little marks on it. Some of these marks are girdle scars, which show where last year's main bud was. By counting the number of girdle scars on a twig, you can tell how old it is.

On a twig there are also little scars that show where the leaves fell off last autumn. If you look carefully with a hand lens or magnifying glass, you will notice tiny holes or pores all over the twig. These are breathing pores called lenticels.

Leaves

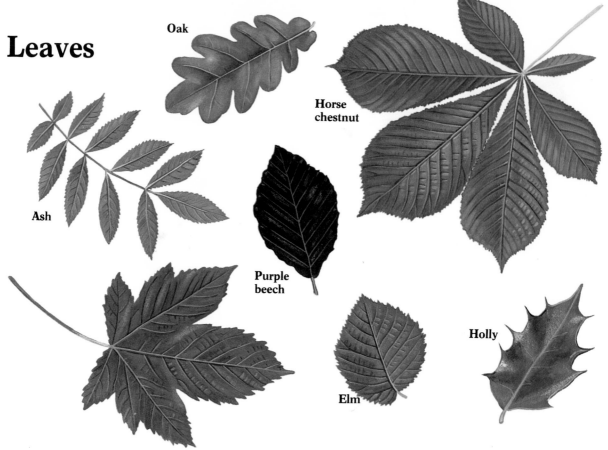

Oak

Horse chestnut

Ash

Purple beech

Elm

Holly

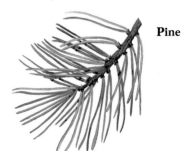

Pine

Each kind of tree has a different shaped leaf. You can recognize most kinds of trees quite easily by their leaves. Most tree leaves are green. But sometimes the green is covered over by another color, such as red. The green substance in leaves is called chlorophyll.

The leaves make food for the tree. To make food they need the water and mineral salts the roots take up from the soil. These are carried inside little tubes in the veins of the leaves.

Leaves also need sunshine and a gas from the air called carbon dioxide. The green chlorophyll in the leaves uses the sunshine to turn the water, carbon dioxide and mineral salts into food. Most trees do not grow well in shady places. There is not enough sunlight for the leaves to make their food.

The veins on a chestnut leaf

8

Oak

Losing leaves

Many trees lose all their leaves in the winter. These are called deciduous trees. The oak, ash, elm, maple, beech and apple are some common deciduous trees. Deciduous trees grow new leaves in the spring.

Some trees keep their leaves in the winter. They are called evergreens. The holly, yew, pine and laurel are common evergreen trees. The leaves of evergreen trees do not last forever. They fall off a few at a time throughout the year. If you look underneath an evergreen tree, you will see some of the leaves that have fallen.

Ash

Beech

Elm

Yew

Holly

Laurel

Maple

Apple

Flowers

Most trees have flowers. Some tree flowers, such as those of the horse chestnut, apple, cherry and hawthorn, are beautiful. They are brightly colored flowers that attract insects. But other tree flowers, like those of the oak, beech and ash, are small and easily missed.

We call the flowers of many trees catkins. Hazel, willow, alder, poplar and oak flowers are all called catkins.

Crab apple

Flowering cherry

Horse chestnut

Oak

Beech

Ash

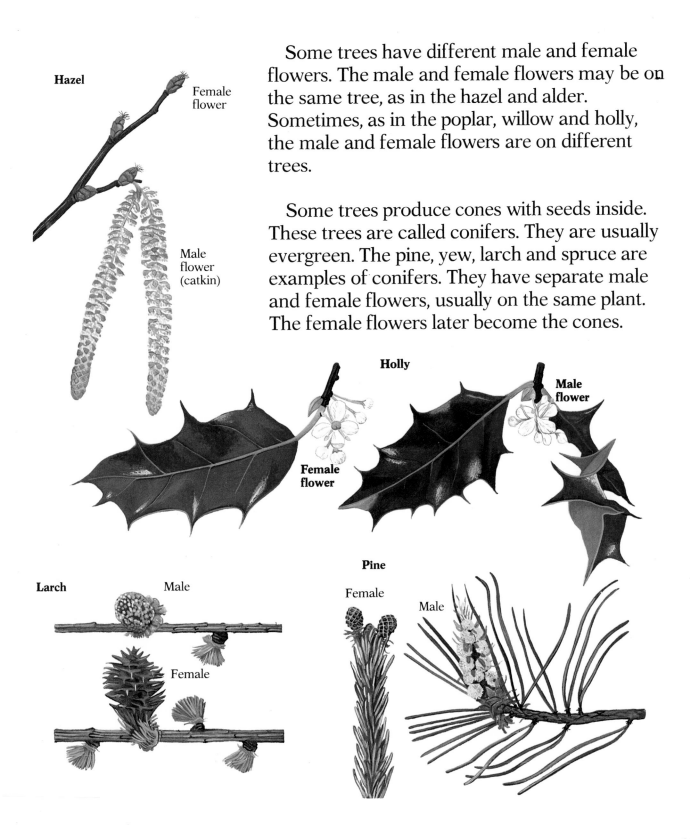

Some trees have different male and female flowers. The male and female flowers may be on the same tree, as in the hazel and alder. Sometimes, as in the poplar, willow and holly, the male and female flowers are on different trees.

Some trees produce cones with seeds inside. These trees are called conifers. They are usually evergreen. The pine, yew, larch and spruce are examples of conifers. They have separate male and female flowers, usually on the same plant. The female flowers later become the cones.

Hazel

Female flower

Male flower (catkin)

Holly

Female flower

Male flower

Larch

Male

Female

Pine

Female

Male

Do you remember?

(Look for the answers in the part of the book you have just been reading if you do not know them.)

1 How would you describe a tree?

2 What are the three main parts of a tree?

3 What are very thin branches called?

4 Give three reasons why trees must have roots.

5 How can you tell the age of a tree?

6 What are the little marks on a twig?

7 What is the green substance in leaves called?

8 What things must a leaf have in order to make food for the tree?

9 What do we call a tree that loses all its leaves in winter?

10 Name three evergreen trees.

11 When do evergreen trees lose their leaves?

12 Name three trees that have catkins.

13 What is a conifer?

14 What do the female parts of conifers develop into?

Things to do

1 **Make some model trees.** Use clay to make the trunk. You can use real twigs for the branches. Cut the leaves out of paper and color them.

Paper trees can be made from rolled up newspaper or drawing paper you have colored. Carefully cut along the roll of paper at one end so that the strips form leaves and branches. Which trees do your paper trees most look like?

2 **Make a collection of tree leaves.** Take only one or two of the best leaves from each tree. There are various ways of making a leaf collection. One is to arrange the leaves carefully between sheets of newspaper or blotting paper and to press them under bricks or books for several days. Mount the leaves neatly on sheets of poster board or drawing paper. Label each leaf with the name of the tree.

Another way of making a leaf collection is to make rubbings of each of your pressed leaves. Lay a pressed leaf on the table with the veins uppermost. Place a piece of thin paper over the leaf. Rub a crayon over the paper until you can see the leaf. Cut out the leaf rubbing and stick it in your book or mount it on a sheet of poster board.

Another kind of leaf print can be made by using paint. Lay a pressed leaf on a sheet of newspaper and carefully brush poster paint on the underside of the leaf using a clean brush. Make sure that you paint the veins of the leaf. Place the painted side of the leaf on a clean sheet of drawing paper and carefully cover it with newspaper. Press gently on the newspaper. Lift off the leaf carefully and let the paint dry.

Splatter prints are even more fun to make and look very attractive. You will need some pressed leaves, some thin poster paint, some newspapers, an old toothbrush and a toothpick or some other thin piece of stick.

Cover the table with sheets of newspaper and place a sheet of drawing paper in the center. Arrange your pressed leaves on the drawing paper. Put a little of the thin paint on the toothbrush. Hold the toothbrush, bristles downwards, over the drawing paper and rub the bristles with the tooth-pick. This scatters the paint over the paper. Keep doing this until all the paper is covered with paint spots. When the paint is dry, carefully remove the leaves.

One way of preserving leaves is to coat them with wax. Ask a grown-up to melt some old candles or paraffin wax (you can buy this at a drugstore) for you in an old saucepan. The wax should only just melt, it must not boil. Pick up a leaf by its stalk and quickly lower it into the molten wax, and pull it out again right away. Hold the leaf for a few minutes until the wax has set.

Make a display of your waxed leaves for the nature table. Every leaf should be labeled with the name of the tree it came from.

You might also try to preserve flowers in wax. Perhaps you could make a collection of preserved tree flowers.

You can make plaster casts of your leaves if you obtain some clay, some newspaper, some poster board, a flat piece of wood, an old jug and some plaster of Paris.

Flatten the clay into a smooth sheet about ½" thick and big enough to hold the leaf. Place the leaf on the clay with the veins downwards. Cover the leaf with paper and press it hard with the piece of wood. If you can obtain one, an old rolling pin is ideal to flatten the clay and to press the leaf into it.

Take the paper away and carefully remove the leaf without touching the clay any more than necessary. You should now have a mold of the leaf in the clay. Put a strip of poster board about 1½" wide around the mold. Fasten the ends with clear tape or a paper clip.

Put a small quantity of water in the old jug. Carefully spoon plaster of Paris into the water and stir it with a clean stick or another spoon. (Do not get any water in the bag of plaster.) Add plaster of Paris to the water until the mixture has the same thickness as custard. Slowly and carefully pour the liquid plaster into the mold. Tap

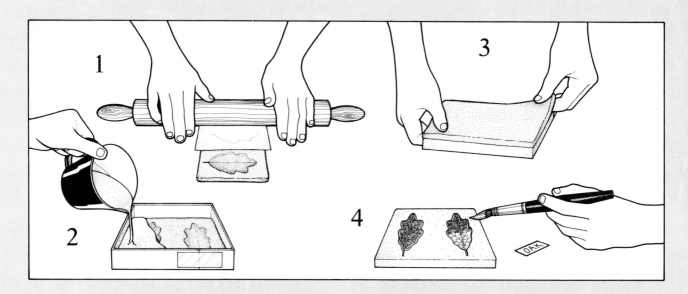

the mold gently to remove any air bubbles, which will weaken the plaster when it sets.

Leave the plaster for several hours to dry — to leave it overnight is best. Peel off the poster board and clay. Paint your plaster cast with poster paint or emulsion paint. Label each of your plaster casts with the name of the tree the leaf came from.

You might try to make plaster casts of small twigs as well.

3 Study your collection of leaves. Try to find out as much as you can about it. Which is the largest leaf? Which is the smallest? Which is the thinnest and which the thickest? Which leaves have smooth edges, which toothed or crinkled edges? Which leaves are made up of smaller leaflets? Which leaves have the most veins? Which leaf has the most colors? Which kinds of leaves have most often been eaten by insects and other animals?

Keep a small notebook in which to write all you have discovered about leaves.

4 Make sets to show which trees are evergreen, which are deciduous and which are conifers. Draw three large circles and write the words "evergreen," "deciduous" and "conifers" beside them. Now put the names of as many trees as you can in the right circles.

Which circle has the most trees in it? Are there any trees that appear in more than one set? Write about what you have learned from your sets.

5 Write a story about a magic tree. One day a witch left her broomstick standing in a wood while she picked toadstools for a magic spell. When she went back for her broomstick, the witch could not find it. Later the broomstick grew into a tree. It was a tree that no one had ever seen before. Its leaves, branches and flowers all had magic powers.

Make up a story about what happened to the tree. Draw some pictures to illustrate your story.

6 Find out the story of a tree. If a tree could talk, it would have an exciting story to tell. To discover the story of a tree for yourself you will need a large log or a section of a really old tree. If you cannot obtain either of these, try to find a large tree stump. Sandpaper the cut surface of the stump until it is clean and smooth. Place a large sheet of waxed paper over the stump of the tree. Rub over the paper with a wax crayon until all the annual rings show up.

We already know how to tell the age of a tree by counting the annual rings. The ring on the outside of the log, section or tree stump will be the year in which the tree was felled. Find out what year that was.

When you know the date of the outside ring, count each ring into the center and you will know the year in which the tree began its life.

Begin at the center of the tree and mark every tenth ring with its date, using black India ink. If the rings are wide, you could mark the date on every ring.

When you have marked the dates on the tree, you could read books to find out what happened during the tree's life. Here are some things you could find out:
Changes in the clothes people wore, their food and their houses.
Changes in transport — ships, trains, cars, airplanes, bicycles.
When such things as radio, television, cameras and telephones were invented.
Which presidents were in office.
Which wars were fought.

What famous events took place.
When you and the members of your family were born.
Make little flags fixed to pins and stick them in the annual ring for the year in which these things happened. Write and draw pictures about all your discoveries.

7 Carry out a survey of your local trees. Make a large sketch-map of the area around your home or school. Write in the names of the streets. Draw in landmarks such as churches, schools, shops and parks.

Now carefully draw in small colored circles showing where trees are growing. Write the name of the tree inside each circle.

Which trees are the most common? Why have these particular kinds of trees been grown? How did they get there?

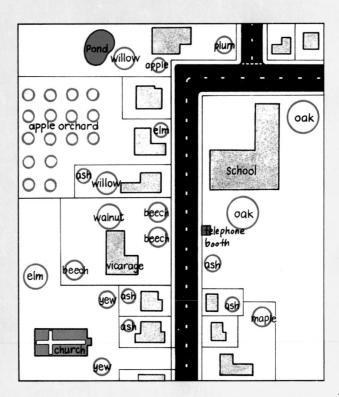

Fruits and seeds

Each kind of tree has a different kind of fruit with seeds in it. The fruit develops from the flower.

An apple is the fruit of the apple tree. Inside the apple are the seeds, which can grow into a new apple tree. The acorn is the fruit of the oak tree. Inside it is a seed from which a new oak tree can grow.

Some tree seeds are scattered by animals and birds. Acorns, hazelnuts, apple seeds and elderberries are just four examples. The animal may hide the fruits and not be able to find them again. This often happens with acorns and hazelnuts. Or the animal or bird may eat the soft parts of the fruit and drop the seeds. This happens to apple seeds and elderberries.

Apple

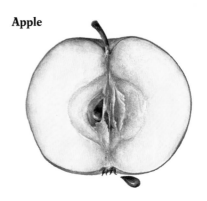

Grey squirrel hiding nuts

Food from the forest

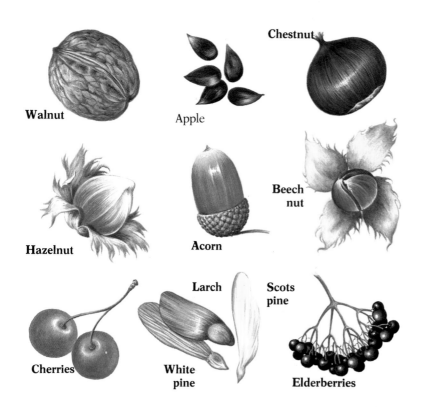

Walnut

Apple

Chestnut

Hazelnut

Acorn

Beech nut

Cherries

White pine

Larch

Scots pine

Elderberries

16

Many tree seeds have wings and are blown along by the wind. Pine, birch, linden and maple are just a few examples.

Ash

Norway maple

Elm

Linden

English elm

Sugar maple

Winged seeds

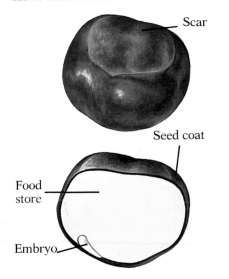

Horse chestnut seed

Scar

Seed coat

Food store

Embryo

Every tree fruit has one or more seeds that can grow into new trees. The seeds are all sizes and shapes. But they are alike in two ways. Each contains a tiny plant called an embryo. All the seeds also contain some food that helps the embryo plant to start growing. The hard coat on the outside of the seed protects the embryo from harm.

If you look closely at a seed you will find a little mark. This is a scar. The scar shows where the seed was joined to the inside of the fruit.

Germination

When the seed starts to grow, it swells as it takes in moisture. Then the embryo inside starts to grow. The skin of the seed splits and a little white root appears. The root pushes its way down through the soil. Next, a white shoot pushes upwards. Soon, when it is above ground, the shoot grows green leaves like those of the parent tree. Until this time the seedling has not been able to make any food for itself. It was fed by two thick leaves inside the seed. This happens in many tree seeds such as those of oak, walnut and horse chestnut.

In some other seeds, such as maple, beech, hawthorn and holly, the two leaves inside the seed get pushed up above the soil. They open up and turn green, and begin to make food for the seedling. The leaves that come later are like those of the parent tree.

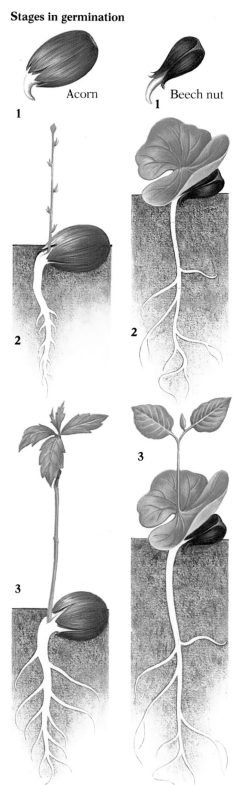

Stages in germination

Acorn

Beech nut

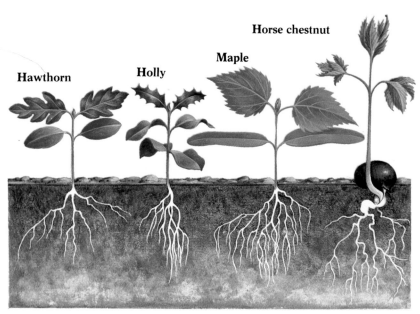

Hawthorn

Holly

Maple

Horse chestnut

18

Seedlings and saplings

Slug

Very few seeds ever last long enough to begin to grow. Large numbers are eaten by birds and animals during the winter. Many tree seeds do not find a suitable place to grow. Even if the seeds do fall onto moist soil, a lot are eaten by slugs, millipedes and other small animals. Many animals like to eat tree seedlings. Of the thousands of acorns produced by a large oak tree, for example, only a few seedlings will survive.

Young trees are called saplings. Even the saplings are not safe from animals. Mice, voles, squirrels, rabbits, hares and deer will all eat the bark or leaves of sapling trees.

So, of all the seeds produced by a large tree, perhaps only one or two saplings will survive. But it does not really matter, since a tree may live for hundreds of years and has plenty of time to produce more of its own kind.

Rabbit

Deer

19

Stages in leaf fall of a maple tree

1

2

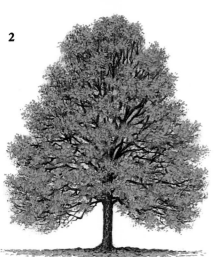

3

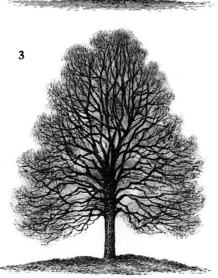

Winter is a difficult time for trees. As the weather becomes colder in the autumn, the tree roots find it harder to get enough water. Most of the water they take up is used by the trunk and branches. There is less and less for the leaves. Gradually the leaves of deciduous trees become dry. The leaves change color, often becoming beautiful shades of red, brown, orange or yellow. In time, the leaves fall off the deciduous trees, leaving scars on the twigs.

The leaves of evergreen trees are thick and tough. They can hold water for a longer time. Very little of the water taken up by the roots of evergreen trees goes into the air. So the leaves of evergreen trees can stay alive during the winter.

Beech

Oak

Sycamore

Elm

Ash

Bay

Not to scale

Decay

When leaves fall from a tree, they lie on the ground. Gradually they decay or rot away. Animals, such as earthworms, and tiny living things in the soil break down the substances that make up the leaves. The most important tiny living things to break down the leaves are bacteria.

In time, the leaves are changed to mineral salts in the soil. The mineral salts help to produce food for plants. They act as a natural fertilizer. All kinds of plants, including trees, take up the mineral salts and use them to help them grow.

When other parts of the tree fall, including the trunk, branches and twigs, they too slowly decay away. They also form mineral salts that other plants can use as a food.

A rotting log

Worm pulling leaf into burrow

Importance of trees

Picking apples

Trees are very important. They provide food and nesting places for many birds and amimals. Trees produce fruits and nuts for humans to eat. They purify the air we need to breathe. They make our gardens and the countryside look attractive. Trees also give shelter from the weather for crops and farm animals. They stop the soil from being washed or blown away.

Trees provide us with wood or lumber. Man has used the wood of trees for thousands of years. Wood is good for fires and hundreds of things can be made from it.

23

Wood

Different woods are used to make different things. Oak is a very strong wood. It is used to make strong furniture, boats, some kinds of flooring and fences. Once, oak was used to hold up the walls and roofs of houses. Beech wood is used for furniture, some wooden floors and the handles of tools. The wood of some ash trees is used to make baseball bats.

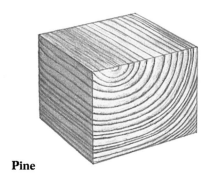
Pine

Much of the United States was once covered with thick forests of oak, maple and other trees. But because we have used so much wood in the past, most of these old forests have now been cleared. The forests have also been cut down to make way for fields, factories, shops, houses and roads.

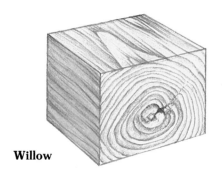
Willow

Clearing trees to make a new road

Beech

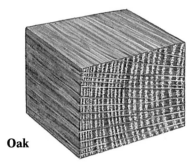
Oak

Pine cabinet

Recently felled pine logs

Beech mallet

Oak chest

Nowadays much of our lumber comes from large planted forests. Most of these forests are of pine, spruce or other conifers. These conifers are planted because they grow quickly. The trunks of these trees are also straight when they are grown close together.

When the trees are between 60 and 120 years old, they are about 100 feet high. The trees are then felled, and the land is cleared and replanted with more trees.

Some of the wood from conifers is used for telephone poles and for building houses. Some is used for making matchsticks. But much is turned into wood pulp. This is used for making paper.

Do you remember?

1   What do tree fruits develop from?

2   What is inside a fruit?

3   What are the two ways in which tree seeds may be scattered?

4   What are two ways in which all seeds are alike?

5   What does the hard coat on the outside of a tree seed do?

6   What is the little mark on the outside of a seed, and what does it show?

7   Why does the seed swell when it starts to grow?

8   Which part of the embryo comes out of the seed first?

9   Why do few tree seeds ever last long enough to grow?

10   What is a sapling?

11   Name some animals that eat saplings.

12   Why is winter a difficult time for deciduous trees?

13   What are the leaves of evergreen trees like?

14   What is another word for "decay"?

15   What are the most important tiny living things that make leaves decay?

16   What are mineral salts used for?

17   In what ways are trees important to animals?

18   Give three reasons why trees are important to humans.

19   What is oak wood used for?

20   What is the wood of conifers used for?

Things to do

1   **Make a collection of tree fruits and seeds.** Do this in the autumn. Label all the fruits and seeds and display them on your nature table.

2   **Collect some fresh cones from under pine trees and other conifers.** If you dry the cones they will open and you will be able to shake out some of the seeds. What do the seeds look like? How do you think the seeds are normally scattered?

Paint the cones to make table decorations. You could use the cones with matchsticks, acorns, walnuts and other tree fruits and seeds to make model animals.

3   Make a wax relief picture of a tree. Use a candle or a wax crayon to draw the shape of a tree on a sheet of paper. Now paint over the whole sheet of paper using a bright color such as red or orange. When the picture is dry, you can mount it on construction paper or stick it in your workbook.

4   Measure the height of some trees. Begin by using a tape measure to see how tall a friend is. Then ask your friend to stand under the tree you wish to measure. Now stand far enough away so that you can see both your friend and the top of the tree.

Hold a pencil at arm's length and move your thumb until the piece of pencil you have uncovered seems to be the same height as your friend. Now see how many times that same piece of pencil goes into the height of the tree.

Suppose the piece of pencil goes into the tree 10 times, and your friend is 5 feet tall. Then your tree is 10 times 5 feet, or 50 feet high. Now ask your friend to change places with you to check your measurements.

Use a tape measure or a piece of string and a ruler to measure how far it is around the trunk of the tree. We call this distance the girth of the tree.

Can you find a way to measure how far the branches spread in all directions without climbing the tree?

Which is the tallest tree you can find? How tall is it? Which tree has the biggest girth and the biggest spread of its branches? You might also guess how old you think each tree is.

5   Make a collection of bark rubbings. You will need some thin drawing paper, four thumbtacks, and some wax crayons.

Place a sheet of paper against the bark of a tree and fasten it there with the thumbtacks. Rub over the paper with a wax crayon until the pattern of the bark shows on the paper. Cut out the pattern and mount it on another piece of paper to make a picture. Write the name of the tree on your bark rubbing.

6   Measure tree shadows. Choose a bright, sunny morning to look at a tree that is standing out in the open. Use sticks or stones to mark how far the tree's shadow stretches. Measure the distance from your sticks or stones to the trunk of the tree. Make a sketch-plan to show your tree and its shadow. Look again at the shadow every hour during the day. How does the shadow change? Why does it change?

7   Write a story about a forest. Pretend that you are standing in a pine forest. All around you there are tall trees towering up to the sky. The ground is covered with a thick carpet of pine needles. Describe what you can see, hear, touch and smell.

Include in your story a description of what you think the forest would be like at night.

8 Study the small animals found among dead leaves. Spread some sheets of newspaper over the table and then carefully sort through the dead leaves that collect at the foot of trees or under hedges. Use a magnifying glass or hand lens to examine any small animals you discover. Count how many of each kind there are. Try to find the names of the animals from books.

You might also carefully take a piece of rotting log and look for tiny animals in it. Again, try to identify them and count them.

Be sure to put the animals back under the tree or hedge from which they came when you have finished looking at them.

9 Make a collection of different kinds of twigs. Do this in March or April. Cut a small twig from each kind of tree, being careful not to tear the bark.

Look at the twigs you collect with a hand lens or magnifying glass. What are the buds like? How are they arranged? Can you see any scars on the twigs? Make colored drawings to show what each of your twigs looks like. Find out how long some of your twigs took to grow.

Keep some of the twigs in little jars of water indoors. Draw the leaves as they unfold. How many leaves were packed inside each bud on each kind of twig?

10 Make a collection of songs and poems about trees. Look in song books and poetry books. Copy the songs and poems into a notebook. Write some tree poems of your own to put in the notebook. Draw and color some pictures to go with the poems and songs.

11 Make a list of things that are made partly or completely of wood. Look around your home or school for ideas. Think carefully about each of the things on your list. Are there any materials that could be used instead of wood in the things on your list? Write these down as well.

12 Keep a diary or scrapbook or make a large wallchart about one tree that is near your home or school. Study the tree for a whole year. What kind of tree is it?

Make drawings or paintings, or take photographs, to show your tree in summer and winter. Write down as many measurements as you can for your tree: its height, girth and how far its branches spread, for example. Collect bark rubbings, twigs, and leaves for leaf prints. Press examples of the tree's flowers and mount examples of its fruit.

Draw or paint the birds that visit your tree. You could make a bird calendar and write in the birds you see in your tree each month. Make careful drawings of any insects or other small animals you see on your tree. Write notes about their life histories. Look carefully for any plants growing on your tree. Stick pressed specimens in your book or on your chart.

What is the wood of your tree used for? Can you obtain a small piece of that kind of wood for your book? A carpenter might be able to give you a piece.

Experiments to try

Do your experiments carefully. Write or draw what you have done and what happens. Say what you have learned. Compare your findings with those of your friends.

1 Falling leaves

What you need: A stool, a strong wooden box or a step-ladder; a stop-watch if you have one; some dead tree leaves of different kinds and different sizes.

What you do: Stand on the stool, box or step-ladder with one leaf in each hand. When a friend gives the signal, drop both leaves together. Ask your friend to see which leaf reaches the ground first. The friend can time how long the leaves take to reach the ground with a stop-watch or by counting slowly, starting at the moment you let the leaves go.

Do big leaves fall faster than small ones? Do leaves with a simple shape fall faster than leaves with a more complicated shape? If you cut off the leaf stalk, does the leaf fall faster or slower? Is it the size of a leaf or its weight that decides how fast it falls?

2 How fast do leaves decay?

What you need: Some tree leaves of different kinds; some flowerpots, jam jars or yogurt cups containing moist garden soil; some labels.

What you do: Bury one leaf of each kind just under the surface of the soil in each pot. Label the pots with the names of the tree leaves in them. Put the pots on a warm windowsill and keep the soil moist. Every two weeks, look at the leaves to see how much has decayed away. Then bury the leaves again.

Do some leaves decay faster than others? What happens if you put some leaves in pots outside? Do they decay faster or slower than those indoors?

Try tying small labels onto some leaves. Tie each leaf to a little stick in a flower-bed. Look at the leaves every week and see how fast they decay. Are any of the leaves eaten by animals? Can you find out what kinds of animals eat the leaves? Which kinds of leaves are eaten most?

3 Twigs and water

Twigs kept in pots of water need more water from time to time. Where does it go to?

What you need: Some leafy twigs; jam jars; olive oil, castor oil, cooking oil or some other vegetable oil; sticky labels.

What you do: Put a leafy twig in a jar half-filled with water. Mark how far the water comes up the side of the jar with a sticky label.

Take another twig of the same kind and with the same number of leaves, and stand it in another jar half-filled with water. Again, mark the water level with a sticky label. Then carefully pour a little oil on the water so that it forms a layer 1/4 inch thick on top of the water.

Have another jar half-filled with water, but with no twig in it. Mark the water level.

Half-fill another jar with water. Do not put a twig in it but put a thin layer of oil on the water. Mark the water level on the jar.

Measure the water levels in all four jars every day. Which jar loses the most water? Where does the water go to? Which jar loses the least water? What effect does the oil have? What does the twig do with the water?

Now do the experiment again with just two jars half-filled with water. Put a twig with four leaves on it in one jar, and a twig of the same kind but with eight leaves on it in the other jar. Pour a little oil on the surface of the water in both jars. Which jar loses the most water?

Now compare twigs with large leaves with those with small leaves. Compare twigs from different kinds of trees. Compare evergreen tree twigs with deciduous tree twigs. Which kind takes up the most water, and which the least?

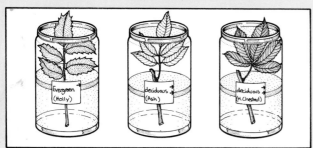

To see where the water goes to, put a large plastic bag over one of the twigs in a jar of water with a layer of oil. What do you see after a day or two?

4   Which tree fruits and seeds do birds like best?

What you need: At least ten tree fruits or seeds of as many different kinds as possible; some old saucers or coffee can lids.

What you do: Do this experiment in the autumn or winter when the birds are hungry. Put out breadcrumbs for the birds on the same part of the playground or lawn every day for several days.

When the birds are used to feeding in the chosen place, arrange the saucers or lids there so that they are all the same distance apart. Put ten fruits or seeds of one kind in one dish, ten of a different kind in another, and so on. Watch carefully from a window to see which birds come to your dishes.

Which kinds of fruits or seeds do the birds eat? How many fruits or seeds of each kind do they eat? Do different birds like different kinds of fruits and seeds?

5   Planting tree seeds

What you need: Flowerpots, yogurt cups or margarine containers; potting soil or soil from under trees; tree fruits and seeds of different kinds — acorns, beech nuts, maple "keys" and horse chestnuts are good ones to start with. Try also elm and ash fruits, if they are still green, and apple and orange seeds.

What you do: Plant one tree seed carefully in each pot of soil. Bury the seeds about 1/4 inch deep. Put the pots on a warm windowsill and keep the soil in the pots moist. Be patient, since some tree seeds are very slow to grow! Record carefully what happens to the seeds in each of your pots. Make drawings to show what the seedlings look like. Measure the seedlings regularly and make graphs to show how they grow.

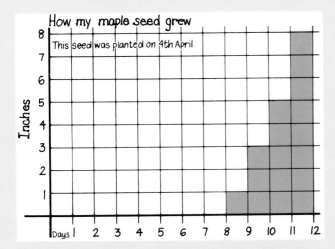

Plant some more tree seeds at different depths in the pots — 1/8 inch, 1/2 inch, 1 inch, and 2 inches are some of the depths you might try. Do the seeds grow?

Plant some seeds upside down and some on their sides. Do they grow?

Keep some pots containing seeds planted the right way up in a warm room and some out of doors in the cold. Keep some more pots in the light and some in the dark. Make sure the soil in all the pots stays moist. Make notes or drawings to show what happens in each experiment. What have you learned about growing tree seeds?

6 Experiments with wood

What you need: Small blocks or scraps of different kinds of wood (perhaps from a carpenter); a large bowl; a hammer and some small nails; scales; poster paint and a brush; a magnifying glass.

What you do: Look at the different kinds of wood with a hand lens or magnifying glass. Look at the different patterns or grain on them. Wet each of the blocks of wood with water. Describe what happens to the appearance of each of them.

Try floating the blocks of wood in a bowl of water. Which kinds float the best? Do any kinds sink?

Weigh some of the blocks of wood before you float them. Leave them in the water for a day or two. Then wipe them dry and weigh them again. Which kinds of wood have taken up the most water?

Find out which of the blocks of wood is the hardest and which the softest. Do this work in the playground, or on an old table or a carpenter's bench. Carefully hammer a nail into each of the blocks of wood.

Which block of wood does a nail go into easiest and which is the hardest to get a nail into? Which wood is the easiest to scratch with a nail and which is the hardest?

Mix some poster paint and paint your blocks of wood. Which kind is the easiest to paint and which the hardest? Why are some of the blocks of wood hard to paint?

If you had big pieces of wood of all the kinds you have used in these experiments, which would you use to make a workbench? Which wood would it be easiest to use for wood carving? Say why you would use the kind of wood you have chosen in each case.

Glossary

Here are the meanings of some words that you might have met for the first time in this book.

Annual rings: the rings to be seen on the cut stump of a tree or on a log. They show how much the tree grew each year and also how old it is.

Bacteria: tiny living things too small to be seen without a powerful microscope. Many bacteria cause materials to decay away; a few cause diseases.

Bark: the layer of soft material around the trunk of a tree that protects the layers underneath.

Carbon dioxide: a gas in the air that is used by green plants to make their food.

Catkin: a name given to the long, tail-like flowers of some trees such as oak, hazel, willow and poplar.

Chlorophyll: the green substance that gives plants their coloring, and with which they trap sunlight to help make their food.

Conifer: a tree that does not have flowers although it does have separate male and female parts. The female part develops into a cone that contains seeds. Most conifers have needle-shaped leaves like those of pine or spruce trees.

Crown: the name given to the part of a tree above the trunk. The crown is made up of branches, twigs and leaves.

Decay: to rot away.

Deciduous tree: a tree that loses its leaves in the autumn and grows new ones the following spring.

Embryo plant: the tiny plant within a seed.

Evergreen tree: a tree that does not lose all its leaves in the autumn but, instead, loses them a few at a time throughout the year.

Fruit: the part of the flower that ripens and contains the seeds.

Girth: the distance around the trunk of a tree.

Lenticel: a tiny breathing hole or pore in a twig.

Mineral salts: the chemical substances that trees and other plants obtain from the soil and use as food.

Sapling: the name given to a young tree.

Seed: the small object within a fruit that grows into a new plant.

Timber: the name given to the wood of a tree.

Tree: a large, woody plant.

Trunk: the large, woody stem of a tree.

Acknowledgments

The publishers would like to thank the following for permission to reproduce transparencies:

Bruce Coleman Ltd: J Burton p. 3 and cover (left), E Crichton p. 23, M P L Fogden p. 3 and G Langsbury p. 16 (bottom); Heather Angel: p. 22 (top and bottom), p. 24, p. 25 and cover (center); Oxford Scientific Films: p. 16 (top) and p. 22 (center); ZEFA/K Benser: p. 20.

Index